D0094393

42

THE
BEST
QUESTION
EVER

?

STUDY GUIDE

ANDY STANLEY

Multnomah® Publishers *Sisters, Oregon*

THE BEST QUESTION EVER STUDY GUIDE
published by Multnomah Publishers, Inc.
© 2004 by North Point Ministries, Inc.

International Standard Book Number: 1-59052-462-4

Interior design and typeset by Katherine Lloyd, The DESK

Unless otherwise indicated, Scripture quotations are from:
The Holy Bible, New International Version
© 1973, 1984 by International Bible Society,
used by permission of Zondervan Publishing House

Other Scripture quotations are from:
New American Standard Bible (NASB)
© 1960, 1977 by the Lockman Foundation
The Living Bible (TLB) © 1971.
Used by permission of Tyndale House Publishers, Inc.
All rights reserved.

Multnomah is a trademark of Multnomah Publishers, Inc.,
and is registered in the U.S. Patent and Trademark Office.
The colophon is a trademark of Multnomah Publishers, Inc.

Printed in the United States of America

For information:
MULTNOMAH PUBLISHERS, INC.
POST OFFICE BOX 1720
SISTERS, OREGON 97759

05 06 07 08 09 10—10 9 8 7 6 5 4 3 2 1

Contents

Foolproof

by Andy Stanley

We've all made dumb decisions. No matter who you are, this is something we all have in common. There are purchases we wish we hadn't made, loans we regret signing up for, people we wish we hadn't dated, parties we wish we hadn't gone to, jobs we wish we hadn't taken…the list goes on. In some cases, the implications are more serious—marriages we shouldn't have entered into, emotions we wish we had controlled, or drugs we wish we'd never tried. Everybody has made choices they wish they could go back and undo.

In hindsight, it's a little easier to see our mistakes. Oftentimes we vow never to make mistakes like that again. In some cases, we may wonder how we could have been so deceived. We look back and think, *How could I have been so foolish?*

It could be argued that we're all a little farsighted when it comes to making dumb decisions. When we see someone else about to make a bad choice, it's easy to see it coming. It's obvious. But somehow, when it's up close and personal, the issues get foggy. Emotions cloud our vision. Circumstances pressure our thinking. And the next thing we know, we have made a decision we regret.

Imagine if we could learn to see clearly *before* we make some of our dumb decisions. That's not only something we desire; it's what God wants for us as well. And it's not as unattainable as we might think. As we're about to discover in the next several weeks together, wisdom is the key to foolproofing yourself against bad decisions. As you've probably learned by now, it's not enough just to know the dos and don'ts of Scripture. When it comes to sorting out the complexities of each unique situation we face, only wisdom can reveal the best path. And once we learn how to find it, we will have found an approach to life that is foolproof.

—*Andy Stanley*

The Best Question Ever

INTRODUCTION

Every time we make a decision, it is preceded by a series of questions. Sometimes we ask them out loud; sometimes we simply process them in our subconscious. We ask questions like "How much can I afford?" "What are the risks?" "How will this feel?" "How much will I make?" "How much could I lose?" "What are my chances?" Whether you realize it or not, the questions you ask yourself eventually determine your decision.

As a general rule, people operate by two primary tenets: First, we want to get the most out of life; and second, we want to avoid getting into trouble. Therefore, as we evaluate our options in a decision, we tend to focus on whether or not our choices will violate any rules or commandments. If they don't, we often assume they are acceptable. Whether it's a financial decision, a moral choice, a business move, or a relationship, our tendency is to see how close we can get to the edge— and then make our decision accordingly.

But with this approach, many Christians simply ask the wrong questions. According to Scripture, the question is not whether something is moral, ethical, legal, or harmful. For Christians, there's another question that's even more important than those. In this session, we'll discover the Best Question Ever when it comes to making decisions that can impact our lives.

RULES OF ENGAGEMENT

Imagine a major magazine is doing a celebrity profile of you. They are collecting interesting tidbits about you that capture who you are and how you think. They want to know your favorite food, your fondest memory, your philosophy for relationships, and your ideas on politics. As part of their brief bio, they ask you to name the three criteria you use to make all your personal decisions. How would you answer? Write these three criteria in the space below. Discuss your answers among the group.

> *(Example: 1. Does it leave the world better than I found it?*
> *2. What does the Bible say about it? 3. Is it the right thing*
> *at this point in my life?)*

EXERCISE

1.

2.

3.

EXERCISE

VIDEO NOTES

From the video message, fill in the blanks.

1. The question we must begin to ask is: "Is it the
   _____ thing for me to do?"

> " *If you're asking the
> wrong question,
> it doesn't matter what
> the answer is.* "

DISCUSSION QUESTIONS

Take a few moments to discuss your answers to these questions with
the group.

1. We all make dumb decisions. Give examples of some of
   the really dumb decisions you've seen people make.

2. What are some of the reasons we make unwise decisions?

3. Recall a wise decision you have made and how that impacted your life.

4. What is a foolish decision you have made that caused you regret?

5. What decision are you considering now, and how has this discussion affected your thinking?

6. In what specific area of your life do you need the wisdom of God?

NOTES

MILEPOSTS

■ When making decisions, our tendency is to ask, "What is acceptable?"

■ Paul encourages his readers to ask, "What is the wise thing to do?"

■ The key to making wise decisions is to understand the will of the Lord.

WHAT WILL YOU DO?

In the space below, list at least one decision you are considering now or anticipate in the future. In response to this discussion, what will be your criteria for deciding?

THINK ABOUT IT

If you had to name one specific area of your life in which you need the wisdom of God, what would it be? Name one step you could take to begin experiencing His wisdom in that area.

CHANGING YOUR MIND

As you become familiar with God's Word, it becomes easier to recall His wisdom. There are verses at the end of each session that we hope you will take time to commit to memory.

> Be very careful, then, how you live —
> not as unwise but as wise,
> making the most of every opportunity,
> because the days are evil.
>
> EPHESIANS 5:15

Last Week...

We learned the importance of asking the right questions. Specifically, we saw that decisions should not be made based only on what is permissible. Instead, we should ask, "What is the wise thing to do?"

Session 2

Musical Chairs

INTRODUCTION

In the last session, we discovered the Best Question Ever: "What is the wise thing to do?" This question goes way beyond "Is it right or wrong?" or "What does the Bible say?" This question cuts through all the layers and demands that we be honest about ourselves as individuals— because what's right for somebody else might not be the wise thing for you personally.

Such a penetrating question usually elicits a strong response. Some will respond by embracing wisdom. But for those who don't, there are three typical reactions to wisdom. And each of these reactions is described in detail in the Bible. These responses can be likened to chairs representing our position on wisdom. They indicate our potential responsiveness to instruction. The chair we sit in determines how we will react when confronted with wisdom.

In this session, we'll examine these three chairs and the attitudes they represent. You will have the opportunity to recognize your own tendencies when it comes to applying wisdom. Once you know how to identify yourself as described in Scripture, you will be better equipped to get up from your chair and move toward the seat of wisdom.

Take a Seat

Imagine you are facing an important decision in unfamiliar territory. Examine the following "chairs," or profiles, and consider which one best describes your attitude when faced with a situation like this. Take a seat in the chair that most represents you. Discuss your answers with the group.

a. Regardless of the details, I am confident that everything will work out fine. With my natural skills and instincts, I can usually make a good choice. I am a capable decision maker.

EXERCISE

b. I may not make the perfect choice every time, but at least I know what I want. I take life one day at a time. Nobody's perfect. I make decisions I can live with, and I live with my decisions.

c. In an important situation, personal preference is very important and my decision should reflect my individual needs. There are many opinions, but I don't want anyone else telling me what I should do.

d. I am somewhat concerned. There is a lot riding on my decision and I want to make the best choice. I feel a strong need to collect more information and possibly to consider the opinions of several other people.

VIDEO NOTES

From the video message, fill in the blanks:

1. The naive person lacks _____.

2. The foolish person knows the difference between right
   and wrong, but just doesn't _____.

3. The scoffing person is _____ of those
   who promote wisdom.

> " Your natural response
> to correction says more
> about you than the fact that
> you needed correction. "

DISCUSSION QUESTIONS

Take a few moments to discuss your answers to these questions with
the group.

1. What is the difference between a naive person, a fool, and
   a scoffer (use personal examples)?

2. What is an example of a naive decision? A careless decision? A scoffing decision?

3. At what times in your life have you sat in each of the
   chairs?

4. What steps did you take to get out of each chair?

5. Name a few of the obstacles that are most likely to keep you from moving to the seat of wisdom.

6. Think about one decision you are facing. What needs to happen for you to do the wise thing?

NOTES

MILEPOSTS

- The Bible describes three types of people who fail to embrace wisdom—the naive, the fool, and the scoffer.

- Your reaction to wisdom helps to reveal what it will take for you to receive instruction.

- The naive overcomes foolishness through experience; the fool overcomes foolishness through consequences; the scoffer overcomes foolishness only through a radical change of heart.

WHAT WILL YOU DO?

When you make avoidable mistakes, is it usually because of naïveté, foolishness, or scoffing? This week identify one avoidable mistake from your past, and analyze which of these three obstacles kept you from choosing to do the wise thing.

THINK ABOUT IT

Knowing what you know about your personality, which of the three chairs described in this session would you be most likely to revisit during a weak moment in the future? What is one step you can take this week to begin guarding against such a mistake?

CHANGING YOUR MIND

Old patterns require that we retrain our thinking process. Use this week's memory verse to begin shaping your thinking.

> How long will you simple ones love your
> simple ways? How long will mockers delight in
> mockery and fools hate knowledge?
>
> PROVERBS 1:22

LAST WEEK...

> We learned about three alternatives to being wise. We also saw what it takes for each to escape foolishness and begin to receive instruction.

Session 3

Living on the Edge

INTRODUCTION

No area is more ravaged by the consequences of foolishness than that of morality. You can mishandle your finances, neglect your health, or squander your profession, but somehow when you cross the line morally, the consequences reach deeper and last longer than any other type of failure. One bad moral decision can follow you the rest of your life. From broken homes to pregnancies out of wedlock, from lifelong diseases to mental images that replay temptations relentlessly, the fallout from moral compromise is unforgiving.

For this reason, God gives very specific advice for foolproofing ourselves morally. Because of the extreme danger in this area, He suggests extreme measures to protect us from harm. And while the solution is simple, it isn't easy. God knows all too well the pain He longs to help us avoid.

In this session, we'll learn a simple but powerful technique to guard against moral failure.

Too Close for Comfort

The margins we set for ourselves typically correspond to the risk involved. Review the scenarios below, and indicate your personal comfort zones by answering each question.

1. If you were taking flying lessons, what would be the ideal age requirement for your instructor?

    a. 16

    b. 26

    c. 36

    d. 56

    e. 86

EXERCISE

2. You are on an interstate trip in your car. If the speed limit is 55, what is the ideal speed to expedite your trip while avoiding a ticket?

    a. 45

    b. 55

    c. 65

    d. 85

3. Your car breaks down on a warm summer night, forcing you to walk through an area of the city that is known for crime. A half mile from your destination, you observe someone in a ski mask following you. Would you:

    a. Stop

    b. Continue walking

    c. Jog

    d. Run!

EXERCISE

VIDEO NOTES

From the video message, fill in the blanks.

1. Every wrong moral decision is preceded by a series of

    _____ decisions.

2. God's advice for avoiding moral failure is to

    "_____!"

3. Sexual sin is in a category by _____.

> " Can a man hold fire
> against his chest
> and not be burned?
> PROVERBS 6:27, TLB "

DISCUSSION QUESTIONS

Take a few moments to discuss your answers to these questions with the group.

1. What influences does our culture use to push us over the moral edge?

2. How is sexual sin different from other sins?

3. Who has influenced or set the moral line in your life?

4. When have you ignored the flags of your conscience and made an unwise decision?

5. Does "Runnnn!" seem like a reasonable solution? Why or
   why not?

6. What are you doing to guard against sexual sin?

NOTES

MILEPOSTS

■ Sexual sin is in a category by itself.

■ The key to foolproofing against moral failure is to set a standard so high that, if violated, there would be no consequences.

WHAT WILL YOU DO?

How far would you go to protect what is most valuable to you? This week, take a personal inventory of everything and everyone who would suffer if you experienced moral failure.

THINK ABOUT IT

Where are you most vulnerable to moral failure? What extreme measures can you adopt so that even if you fail, there will be no consequences?

CHANGING YOUR MIND

The authority of God's Word builds on the concept of trust. Train your mind to this principle by meditating on this week's verse over the next few days.

> Flee from sexual immorality. All other sins
> a man commits are outside his body,
> but he who sins sexually sins against his own body.
>
> 1 CORINTHIANS 6:18

LAST WEEK...

We examined the far-reaching effects of foolishness in the arena of morality. Along the way, we discovered practical ways to apply the Bible's instructions to "flee."

Session 4

Time Bandits

INTRODUCTION

Time is the irreducible minimum of life. When you boil life down to its basic components, time is your core commodity. You can run out of money, you can run out of opportunities, and you can run out of luck. But when you run out of time, your life is over.

Therefore, you can't foolproof your life without giving serious thought to how you spend your time. Everyone is allotted a certain number of days in this world. But while many of us focus on how much time we have left, the question we should be asking is, "What are we doing with our time?" Because when you get to the end, success or failure will be largely impacted by how you spent your time.

There is a principle that has the potential to leverage small amounts of your time for the greatest amount of impact. Whether you realize it or not, you've already experienced the effects of this principle in your life. Sometimes it's leveraged for bad and sometimes for good. In this session, we'll look at how you can begin to make small investments that will leverage your time for larger-than-life results.

LEVERAGE

Sometimes the little things have the greatest impact. One good habit, however small, can have a tremendous effect over the course of your lifetime. For each of the following four categories, name one small investment that, if made consistently, would make a positive impact in your life.

   1. Physical:

EXERCISE

2. Relational:

3. Professional:

EXERCISE

4. Spiritual:

VIDEO NOTES

From the video message, fill in the blanks.

1. There is a ___*cumulative*___ value in investing small amounts of time in certain activities over a long period.

2. ___*Neglect*___ has a cumulative value as well.

3. There are rarely immediate ___*consequences*___ for neglecting single installments of time in any particular arena of life.

4. There is no cumulative value in the ___*urgent*___ things we allow to interfere with what's most important to us. *(we don't count what we did instead)*
   . dinner with family
   . note - "urgent but not important"

5. In the ___*critical*___ arenas of life, you cannot make up for lost time.

   ↳ there are
   no all-nighters

   ↳ you cannot cram
   and have healthy
   relationships.

> " *Time can be your worst enemy or your closest ally.* "

DISCUSSION QUESTIONS

Take a few moments to discuss your answers to these questions with
the group. *· seek word ; redeeming the time.*

Great - tangible ✓

1. Why is it so easy to neglect the important things in life?

Investing vs spends ✓

- *people / forces in society are very pervasive*
- *~~failure have to~~*
  fear failure at work

email

- *overvalue time for others thinking I need lots*
  of "me" time: not honestly measuring that.
- *because there are multiple impt. things to*
  pursue.
- *assume there are going to be there...*
- *lack of disaplu...*

2. In what areas of life have you observed the cumulative
effect of neglect?

- *cannot make up for lost time*
- *pray as a couple*
- *finances*
- *time for no #1 friend*

3. What urgent things crowd out the important things in
   your life?

   90/100 — 30% unpredictable interruptions

   — less capacity

   — "feel productive —70% at capacity

   — "is this work worth paying for?"
   (deli slicer). ...
   (loses lesson quality)

4. How have you tried to "make up for lost time"?

   dull / busy.

   · *Low: unclear / number up*
   · *Discipline relational time ... Adam*
   · *Plan prayer*
   · *Rehab - time to pray.*

5. In what area of life do you wish you were using time more wisely?

6. Name one thing you can begin doing consistently to make the most of your time.

· saying no ; yes to self
· work thing : how much do I read...
↗· small limit per day
↗· time per day for reading
· sitting with cords
↗"departure" time

NOTES

MILEPOSTS

- Time is life.

- There is a cumulative value when our time is invested in important things.

- There is no cumulative value when our time is invested in urgent things.

- In the critical arenas of life, we cannot make up for lost time.

WHAT WILL YOU DO?

By now you should have identified at least one thing you could begin doing consistently that would have a cumulative value in your life. Please write it again in the space below. Your assignment for this week is simply to be faithful to practice consistency in this one area. Please report your results to the group next week.

THINK ABOUT IT

As we've learned in this session, consistency is the key to wise management of your time. Imagine applying this principle in one or two key areas of your life. How might your life be different? Discuss.

CHANGING YOUR MIND

Chances are, your patterns for how you spend your time were adopted long ago. In order to modify them, you will need to change your thinking. Memorize the verse for this week to help you remember the cumulative value of time invested in important things.

Four things on earth are small,

yet they are extremely wise:

Ants are creatures of little strength,

yet they store up their food in the summer.

PROVERBS 30:24–25

LAST WEEK...

We learned a powerful principle for leveraging small investments of time to produce tremendous results. We also examined the power of consistency to guard your life against foolishness.

Session 5

A Little Help from Our Friends

INTRODUCTION

No matter how wise you are, there will always be a handful of situations in life in which your judgment is either impaired or inadequate. It's just a fact of life. Sometimes it's because the situation is emotionally charged and it's difficult to maintain perspective. Other times it's because the decision requires knowledge that is beyond your area of expertise. Whatever the case, you will lack wisdom from time to time.

The question is, what should you do when wisdom seems to elude you? Should you give up? Give in? Should you just do the best you can? Or does God have something else in mind to provide wisdom in your time of need?

Believe it or not, lacking wisdom is not necessarily a reflection on your intelligence or your spiritual maturity. Sometimes it's just part of God's plan. You see, God created a unique channel of wisdom that has some important secondary benefits as well. This channel encourages believers to depend on each other and serve each other. And in this session, we'll explore how you can leverage this channel for wisdom when all the other sources run dry.

YOU'VE GOT A FRIEND

For each of the scenarios listed below, name the person or people in your life you would consult for advice.

    1. A severe toothache: *dentist*

EXERCISE

EXERCISE

2. An investment decision:

3. A relationship problem:

4. A parenting challenge:

5. A career decision:

6. A spiritual issue:

VIDEO NOTES

From the video message, fill in the blanks.

1. Wise people know when they don't ___know___.

2. Wise people seek wise ___counsel___.

3. No one is so successful that he or she no longer ___needs___ wise counsel.

4. You will never reach your full potential without ___utilizing___ the wisdom of other people.

5. Wise counsel may come from ___unlikely___ sources.

seek outside counsel

? who can I seek for academic counsel?

? someone in ministry?

If they're so smart, then why didn't they ___. (so you ignore or discount the source)

. we already know what they are going to say.

> " Plans fail for lack of counsel, but with many advisers they succeed.
> PROVERBS 15:22 "

DISCUSSION QUESTIONS

Take a few moments to discuss your answers to these questions with the
group.

1. From current events, give examples of private decisions
   that have become public knowledge.

   · Mel Gibson speeding, driving drunk
   Jerry Falwell
   · Ramsay's killer found / confess

   · Abramoff scandle....

2. What are some areas in which we tend to resist the advice
   of others?

   · areas we're too proud to admit we're failing at.
   where we

3. Why do we resist in these specific areas?

   pride.

4. Name a time when you got great advice or counsel from an unlikely source. How did this come about?

5. Describe a bad decision that impacted more than just you.

6. What's the biggest decision facing you today, and to whom will you turn for wise counsel?

NOTES

MILEPOSTS

■ Wise people know when they don't know.

■ Many of the decisions you make independently and privately eventually become known publicly.

■ Wise people involve other wise people on the front end of the decision-making process.

WHAT WILL YOU DO?

Are you facing an important decision? Have you reviewed your options with anyone? In the space below, describe the most significant decision you face currently. Then name two or three people who might lend insight into your situation.

THINK ABOUT IT

Most of our significant decisions eventually become public. In the space below, name at least one decision you made that came to light in a public way.

CHANGING YOUR MIND

God's Word reminds us that no man is an island. Memorize this week's verse to build your confidence to seek counsel next time you face an important decision.

> The way of a fool is right in his own eyes, but a wise
> man is he who listens to counsel.
>
> PROVERBS 12:15, NASB

We learned the value of getting input from others before making important decisions. By going outside ourselves for wisdom, we improve objectivity and broaden the pool of expertise that shapes our judgment.

Session 6

The Best Decision Ever

INTRODUCTION

Throughout this series, we've talked about the Best Question Ever for making foolproof decisions. In this session, we'll discover "the best decision ever" for foolproofing your entire life.

There's something ironic about the way we live. In every arena of life, certain rules govern things. And when it comes to day-to-day living, we recognize and submit to those rules. Sometimes it's recognizing the rules of the road to avoid a collision, or recognizing the rules of our profession in order to succeed. Other times, it's recognizing the rules of our physical bodies to maintain good health. When it comes to functioning in daily life, we're good at recognizing the rules and submitting ourselves to them in order to excel.

However, when it comes to making life decisions, we struggle to recognize and submit ourselves to the Author of life. It's not unique to our generation either. Even Solomon, the wisest man who ever lived, observed this phenomenon in his day. And out of his observations, he points us to the best decision we could ever make to foolproof our lives.

WHO MAKES THE RULES?

A. Arena of Life	B. Who Makes the Rules?
Work	*Example: Your boss, influential coworkers, customers, the economy, competitors, technology, etc.*
Driving a car	

EXERCISE

Relationships	
Money	
Your health	

VIDEO NOTES

From the video message, fill in the blanks.

1. In every arena of life, there are certain _____ that we must know to make wise decisions.

2. Knowing the rules that govern a decision doesn't make the decision for us, but it narrows our _____.

3. In order to make wise decisions, you must _____ to the rules.

4. When it comes to making life decisions, we are often unwilling to submit to the Author of _____.

5. "The fear of the Lord" is recognition and reverence that leads to _____.

> " *The fear of the* LORD
> *is the beginning of wisdom,*
> *and knowledge of the Holy*
> *One is understanding.*
> PROVERBS 9:10 "

DISCUSSION QUESTIONS

Take a few moments to discuss your answers to these questions with the group.

1. What are some "rules" that you submit to every day?

2. Describe a time when you submitted control to someone else and regretted it.

3. What are some of the differences between submitting control to other people and submitting control to God?

4. What are some areas in which you depend on others to know the rules?

5. What is one step you can take now to submit control to God?

NOTES

MILEPOSTS

■ In every arena of life, there are certain rules that must
be observed to make wise decisions.

■ The beginning of all wisdom is the recognition of, and
submission to, the God of heaven.

WHAT WILL YOU DO?

In column A on the next page, briefly summarize the top three decisions you face currently. Can you imagine committing to follow
God's advice before you even know what it is? What's the worst
answer God could give you? Would it be a big "no"? Perhaps He
would say, "Wait." In column B, write what you would consider the
least desirable answer you could get from God. When you are fin-
ished, review your answers. Do you desire to follow God as much as
you desire to do things a certain way?

A. DECISION	B. WORST CASE FROM GOD
1.	
2.	
3.	

THINK ABOUT IT

God promises to work all things together for our good, especially when we cooperate with His wisdom. For each of the scenarios above, try to imagine the "good" ending to each story. Try to imagine how God might use your obedience and reward your faithfulness. You may not understand His entire plan yet, but it will renew your hope that He has one, and it will help you to apply His wisdom, whatever it may be.

A. DECISION	B. OUTCOME OF OBEDIENCE
1.	
2.	
3.	

CHANGING YOUR MIND

Wisdom begins with the recognition of God as the source of wisdom. Memorize this week's verse to help you submit no matter what.

The fear of the LORD is the beginning of wisdom,

and knowledge of the Holy One is understanding.

PROVERBS 9:10

LEADER'S GUIDE

SO, YOU'RE THE LEADER...

Is that intimidating? Perhaps exciting? No doubt you have some mental pictures of what it will look like, what you will say, and how it will go. Before you get too far into the planning process, there are some things you should know about leading a small-group discussion. We've compiled some tried-and-true techniques here to help you.

Leading 101

BASICS ABOUT LEADING

1. **Don't teach...facilitate**—Perhaps you've been in a Sunday school class or Bible study in which the leader could answer any question and always had something interesting to say. It's easy to think you need to be like that, too. Relax. You don't. Leading a small group is quite different. Instead of being the featured act at the party, think of yourself as the host or hostess behind the scenes. Your primary job is to create an environment where people feel comfortable and

to keep the meeting generally on track. Your party is most successful when your guests do most of the talking.

2. **Cultivate discussion**—It's also easy to think that the meeting lives or dies by *your* ideas. In reality, what makes a small-group meeting successful are the ideas of everyone in the group. The most valuable thing you can do is to get people to share their thoughts. That's how the relationships in your group will grow and thrive. Here's a rule: The impact of your study material will typically never exceed the impact of the relationships through which it was studied. The more meaningful the relationships, the more meaningful the study. In a sterile environment, even the best material is suppressed.

3. **Point to the material**—A good host or hostess gets the party going by offering delectable hors d'oeuvres and beverages. You too should be ready to serve up "delicacies" from the material. Sometimes you will simply read the discussion questions and invite everyone to respond. At other times, you may encourage others to share their own ideas. Remember, some of the best treats are the ones your guests will bring to the party. Go with the flow of the meeting, and be ready to pop out of the kitchen as needed.

4. **Depart from the material**—A talented ministry team has carefully designed this study for your small group. But that doesn't mean you should follow every part word for word. Knowing how and when to depart from the material is a valuable art. Nobody knows more about your people than you do. The narratives, questions, and exercises are here to provide a framework for discovery; however, every group is motivated differently. Sometimes the best way to start a small-group discussion is simply to ask, "Does anyone have any personal insights or revelations they'd like to share from this week's material?" Then sit back and listen.

5. **Stay on track**—Conversation is like the currency of a small-group discussion. The more interchange, the healthier the "economy." However, you need to keep your objectives in mind. If your goal is to have a meaningful experience with this material, then you should make sure the discussion is contributing to that end. It's easy to get off on a tangent. Be prepared to interject politely and refocus the group. You may need to say something like, "Excuse me, we're obviously all interested in this subject; however, I just want to make sure we cover all the material for this week."

6. **Above all, pray**—The best communicators are the ones
   who manage to get out of God's way enough to let Him
   communicate *through* them. That's important to keep in
   mind. Books don't teach God's Word; neither do sermons
   or group discussions. God Himself speaks into the hearts
   of men and women, and prayer is our vital channel to
   communicate directly with Him. So cover your efforts in
   prayer. You don't just want God present at your meeting;
   you want Him to direct it.

*We hope you find these suggestions helpful. And we hope you enjoy
leading this study. You will find additional guides and suggestions for each
session in the Leader's Guide notes that follow.*

Leader's Guide Session Notes

SESSION 1: THE BEST QUESTION EVER

KEY POINT

For many Christians, decision making is a simple process of asking whether the Bible says yes or no on an issue. But God calls us to be much more shrewd than that by asking, "What is the wise thing to do?"

EXERCISE—"RULES OF ENGAGEMENT"

The point of this exercise is to help people begin to think about their own decision-making process—what factors do they consider? And why? Since this is the first activity of the first session, it will be your first experience as a group. Encourage people not to overthink this exercise. Tell them to have fun with it. As the leader, your main goal is to break the ice and set an enjoyable tone for the group.

VIDEO NOTES

1. The question we must begin to ask is: "Is it the <u>wise</u> thing for me to do?"

Notes for Discussion Questions

1. We all make dumb decisions. Give examples of some of the really dumb decisions you've seen people make.

   Participants should have fun sharing personal stories and anecdotes. This is an effective icebreaker. Encourage people to share humorous answers. Beware of going too deep too fast with your group, such as sharing a deeply serious example. This could be the first experience in a group for some people. Their greatest fear may be that they will be forced to share personal information or reveal their spiritual shortcomings. Allow them to stay in their comfort zones for now.

2. What are some of the reasons we make unwise decisions?

   This question is a little more thought provoking and may move toward more personal answers. The idea is to move in small increments from nonthreatening discussion to more personal insights and probing questions.

3. Recall a wise decision you have made and how that impacted your life.

   This personal question can be general in nature or very specific. At this early point in the group's life, comfort levels are still your most important consideration. Don't let anyone feel pressured to divulge more than he or she is comfortable with.

4. What is a foolish decision you have made that caused you regret?

   As with the previous question, be aware of people's comfort levels. Some humorous answers here will help ensure that everyone gets an enjoyable impression of the group.

5. What decision are you considering now, and how has this discussion affected your thinking?

   This question introduces the idea of personal application. In a sense, there's no place to hide here. Be especially sensitive to those who may be uncomfortable sharing personal information. You may offer the first answer to demonstrate a nonthreatening response, such as, "I will need a new car soon, and this discussion makes me desire to make a wise decision instead of just getting whatever I want."

6. In what specific area of your life do you need the wisdom of God?

This question is an invitation for people to consider which arenas of life are most important. As a result, it should prompt them to realize the need for wisdom in all arenas.

What Will You Do?

This exercise is intended to create specific application for each participant. Encourage individuals to be very specific. Everyone faces decisions all the time. This exercise will help them practice asking, "What is the wise thing to do?"

Think About It

This exercise is more general in nature, prompting people to consider ongoing practices that could help them apply wisdom on a daily basis.

SESSION 2: MUSICAL CHAIRS

KEY POINT

The Bible describes three types of people who fail to pursue wisdom. Becoming familiar with these three profiles will help participants recognize their own tendencies and take appropriate action to foolproof their lives.

EXERCISE—"TAKE A SEAT"

The profiles in this exercise correspond to the types of people discussed in this session. Answer *a* represents something the naive person might say; *b* represents something the fool might say; *c* represents something the scoffer might say; *d* represents something the wise person might say.

VIDEO NOTES

1. The naive person lacks <u>experience</u>.

2. The foolish person knows the difference between right and wrong, but just doesn't <u>care</u>.

3. The scoffing person is <u>critical</u> of those who promote wisdom.

Notes for Discussion Questions

1. What is the difference between a naive person, a fool, and a scoffer?

   This question is intended to reinforce learning from the message, helping each person to have a useful understanding of these three profiles.

2. What is an example of a naive decision? A careless decision? A scoffing decision?

   Putting the profiles into practice, this question will help the group examine what it looks like to make each type of decision. This will help participants distinguish between them.

3. At what times in your life have you sat in each of the chairs?

   No doubt, everyone has experiences in each of these situations. Recalling them together will help everyone understand each one more thoroughly.

4. What steps did you take to get out of each chair?

Learning to move beyond the chairs is the whole point of this session. Sharing insights will help each person begin to see what it looks like to pursue wisdom from any given situation.

5. Name a few of the obstacles that are most likely to keep you from moving to the seat of wisdom.

The purpose of this question is to help participants begin to identify up front some of the many things that can make us feel trapped. Recognizing these obstacles is the first step to resolving them.

6. Think about one decision you are facing. What needs to happen for you to do the wise thing?

This question is an exercise in applying what has been learned so far.

WHAT WILL YOU DO?

Distinguishing among the three profiles in this session is extremely important, but it can be tricky. This exercise offers more practice to help reinforce the concepts.

THINK ABOUT IT

There is no substitute for a heart that is broken and willing before God. This assignment is an invitation for participants to take a step toward God, confess any obstacles in their relationship with Him, and receive His embrace and His invitation to find wisdom in Him.

SESSION 3: LIVING ON THE EDGE

KEY POINT

Morality is one arena in which the consequences of foolishness can be severe. The wise thing to do is to set standards so high that even if they were violated, there would be no consequences.

EXERCISE—"TOO CLOSE FOR COMFORT"

This exercise is a warm-up to the concept of setting standards that insulate us from the potential for harm or negative consequences.

VIDEO NOTES

1. Every wrong moral decision is preceded by a series of <u>unwise</u> decisions.

2. God's advice for avoiding moral failure is to "<u>Run!</u>"

3. Sexual sin is in a category by <u>itself</u>.

NOTES FOR DISCUSSION QUESTIONS

1. What influences does culture use to push us over the moral edge?

   To succeed in any goal, it is important to be aware of the obstacles that work against you. This question will help participants begin to see the world around them in a different light.

2. How is sexual sin different from other sins?

The Bible clearly explains that moral failure has unique consequences. Answers to this question may be theological, citing Bible verses, or practical, citing some of the physical or psychological consequences of sexual sin.

3. Who has influenced or set the moral line in your life?

The main purpose of this question is to encourage participants to consider their own moral standards. Do they have any? What determines them?

4. When have you ignored the flags of your conscience and made an unwise decision?

The point of this question is that we can all learn from our past by identifying scenarios that set us up for failure. This can help us make wise decisions next time.

5. Does "Runnnn!" seem like a reasonable solution? Why or why not?

This question should prompt the group to discuss practical ways to apply the message of this verse. Encourage participants to share their suggestions.

6. What are you doing to guard against sexual sin?

It all boils down to this. Each person should take whatever steps necessary to guard against sexual sin. This may be different for each person's unique situation and circumstances.

What Will You Do?

When you think about it in terms of what you stand to lose as a result of failure, you become very motivated to guard against sexual sin.

Think About It

This exercise goes a step further, prompting participants to create specific strategies that may even seem extreme, but are appropriate in light of what's at stake.

SESSION 4: TIME BANDITS

KEY POINT

· Time is like the currency of life. Therefore, you must consider how you spend your time if you want to foolproof your life. This session reveals that the important things in life are achieved by practicing consistency in key areas.

EXERCISE—"LEVERAGE"

This exercise will get people thinking about some of the ways small habits, when applied consistently, can greatly impact the most important arenas of life.

VIDEO NOTES

1. There is a <u>cumulative</u> value in investing small amounts of time in certain activities over a long period.

2. <u>Neglect</u> has a cumulative value as well.

3. There are rarely immediate <u>consequences</u> for neglecting single installments of time in any particular arena of life.

4. There is no cumulative value in the <u>urgent</u> things we allow to interfere with what's most important to us.

5. In the <u>critical</u> arenas of life, you cannot make up for lost time.

NOTES FOR DISCUSSION QUESTIONS

1. Why is it so easy to neglect the important things in life?

   Neglect is usually a matter of losing sight of priorities. This question should help expose some of the day-to-day factors that contribute to our clouded vision.

2. In what areas of life have you observed the cumulative effect of neglect?

   The erosive nature of neglect can be better understood when participants identify how it has worked against them in their own lives.

3. What urgent things crowd out the important things in your life?

   Urgency is one of the main enemies of consistency. This is a good question to help participants identify areas where they should pay attention and develop strategies for guarding against urgency.

4. How have you tried to "make up for lost time"?

This question will expose the areas of greatest need for
each person. It also underscores the futility of attempting
to make up for lost time.

5. In what area of life do you wish you were using time more
   wisely?

This question is intended to produce a wish list for participants, helping them to focus in on areas where they
will make improvements.

6. Name one thing you can begin doing consistently to
   make the most of your time.

Encourage baby steps here. If participants can find success in applying consistency in one area, it can provide
very powerful motivation for other areas as well.

WHAT WILL YOU DO?

This exercise takes the application to the next level. At the risk of being repetitive, it asks each person to commit to one step that he or she can take to experience consistency in this week.

THINK ABOUT IT

Consistency is truly the greatest tool for leverage in life. This exercise encourages participants to begin to envision all the different ways consistency could change their lives.

SESSION 5: A LITTLE HELP FROM OUR FRIENDS

KEY POINT

There are two situations in which everyone needs counsel from time to time. First, when objectivity is vulnerable because of emotional factors. Second, when the situation requires expertise beyond our own. God intends for us to rely on each other and to serve each other with counsel.

EXERCISE—"YOU'VE GOT A FRIEND"

There are many different situations in which we need counsel. Some are as practical as consulting a dentist or a doctor. Others aren't as obvious, however. This exercise will help demonstrate that seeking counsel in any arena is simply a wise practice.

VIDEO NOTES

1. Wise people know when they don't <u>know</u>.

2. Wise people seek wise <u>counsel</u>.

3. No one is so successful that he or she no longer <u>needs</u> wise counsel.

4. You will never reach your full potential without <u>utilizing</u> the wisdom of other people.

5. Wise counsel may come from <u>unlikely</u> sources.

NOTES FOR DISCUSSION QUESTIONS

1. From current events, give examples of private decisions that have become public knowledge.

   This question is intended to reinforce the teaching that it is better to be humble before a few wise people of your own choosing than to be exposed as a fool before the whole world.

2. What are some areas in which we tend to resist the advice of others?

   Some areas are more sensitive than others. This question will help participants face up to their own resistance in these areas.

3. Why do we resist in these specific areas?

   Probing deeper, this question will expose the underlying issues that keep us from seeking wise counsel. Whether it's pride or fear, we need to move beyond our resistance.

4. Name a time when you got great advice or counsel from an unlikely source. How did this come about?

   This question reiterates the fact that God doesn't always speak to us in the ways we expect. We need to be humble enough to hear Him regardless of how He speaks.

5. Describe a bad decision that impacted more than just you.

   One of the great secondary reasons for seeking counsel beforehand is that our decisions affect other people and not just ourselves. This question will yield personal examples of this principle.

6. What's the biggest decision facing you today, and to whom will you turn for wise counsel?

   This question is intended to prompt personal application of the teaching. Each person should be able to identify one situation where he or she can practice applying the principle, as well as one friend or resource for counsel.

WHAT WILL YOU DO?

Similar to question 6, this exercise emphasizes the application by turning it into an assignment.

THINK ABOUT IT

To reinforce the teaching, this exercise revisits the notion that most of our decisions are exposed in one way or another.

SESSION 6: THE BEST DECISION EVER

KEY POINT

Wisdom involves submission to God even when it doesn't make sense. But in the heat of the moment, we can hesitate or second-guess the situation. The best decision we could make is to commit to God's ways no matter what.

EXERCISE—"WHO MAKES THE RULES?"

This exercise is a warm-up to the concept that there are rules for every arena of life. The implication is that since we apply many of these rules so well, we should also be able to take the same approach with God and accept His advice as our standard.

VIDEO NOTES

1. In every arena of life, there are certain <u>rules</u> that we must know to make wise decisions.

2. Knowing the rules that govern a decision doesn't make the decision for us, but it narrows our <u>options</u>.

3. In order to make wise decisions, you must <u>submit</u> to the rules.

4. When it comes to making life decisions, we are often unwilling to submit to the Author of <u>life</u>.

5. "The fear of the Lord" is recognition and reverence that leads to <u>submission</u>.

Notes for Discussion Questions

1. What are some "rules" that you submit to every day?

   This question is an extension of the exercise at the beginning of this session. The point is to recall the many ways we obey rules for our benefit every day. The implication is that we should use the same approach to applying God's rules even when it might not "feel" right or when we might not understand everything.

2. Describe a time when you submitted control to someone else and regretted it.

   One of the reasons we struggle to trust God is that other people have proven untrustworthy in the past. We should not allow the unfaithfulness of a person to give us the wrong impression about God.

3. What are some of the differences between submitting control to other people and submitting control to God?

   As a follow-up to question 2, this question will underscore
   the fact that there is a big difference between making ourselves vulnerable to a person and making ourselves
   vulnerable to God.

4. What are some areas in which you depend on others to
   know the rules?

   This question is intended to reiterate the fact that we
   entrust ourselves to others all the time. How much more
   can we entrust ourselves to God?

5. What is one step you can take now to submit control to
   God?

   The purpose of this question is to elicit some step of personal application from each participant.

WHAT WILL YOU DO?

Often the reason we are reluctant to commit our lives completely to God is that we fear the worst. One of the best ways to begin accepting God's direction in life is to consider the possibilities. This exercise will help each person play out the scenario on paper. Chances are, they will conclude that the things they fear the most aren't so fearful after all. At the very least, writing them down encourages us to face our fears.

THINK ABOUT IT

As a continuation of the previous exercise, this assignment reviews the fact that God works everything for good—even the things we fear the most. By envisioning the "good" conclusion of God's work in our lives, we will be more encouraged to trust Him at every step along the way.

The Best Question Ever
by Andy Stanley

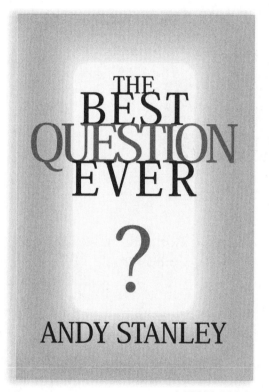

1-59052-390-3

Can you think of a question that has the potential to foolproof your relationships, your marriage, your finances, even your health? A question that, had you asked it and followed its leading, would have enabled you to avoid your greatest regret? Read *The Best Question Ever* to find out how to foolproof your life.

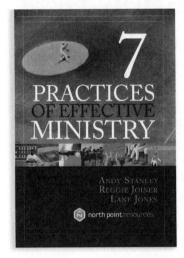

7 PRACTICES OF EFFECTIVE MINISTRY
Andy Stanley, Lane Jones, Reggie Joiner

An insightful and entertaining parable for every ministry leader who yearns for a more simplified approach to ministry.

ISBN: 1-59052-373-3
$19.99 Hardback
Church Resources

CREATING COMMUNITY
Andy Stanley and Bill Willits

Creating Community delivers a successful template for building and nurturing small groups in your church. Andy Stanley and Bill Willits reveal the formula developed over ten years at North Point Community Church, for one of the most successful and admired small group ministries in the country.

ISBN: 1-59052-396-2
$19.99 Hardback
Church Resources

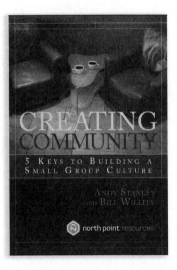

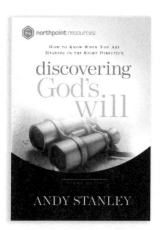

DISCOVERING GOD'S WILL
STUDY GUIDE & DVD

Andy Stanley

God has a personal vision for your life and He wants you to know it even more than you do. Determining God's will can be a difficult process, especially when we need to make a decision in a hurry. In this series, Andy Stanley discusses God's providential, moral, and personal will and how He uses other people and the principles of Scripture to guide us.

STUDY GUIDE 1-59052-379-2, $9.99
DVD 1-59052-380-6, $24.99

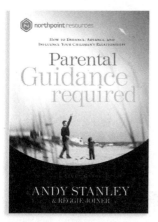

PARENTAL GUIDANCE
STUDY GUIDE & DVD

Andy Stanley and Reggie Joiner

Our lives are influenced by our relationships, experiences, and decisions. Therefore our priority as parents should be to enhance our child's relationship with us, advance our child's relationship with God, and influence our child's relationship with those outside the home.

STUDY GUIDE 1-59052-381-4, $9.99
DVD 1-59052-378-4, $24.99

DEFINING MOMENTS
STUDY GUIDE & DVD

By Andy Stanley

It is no secret that what you don't know CAN hurt you. In spite of that, we still go out of our way at times to avoid the truth. Learn how to discern the truth and apply those "defining moments" in your life with this DVD and study guide.

STUDY GUIDE 1-59052-464-0, $9.99
DVD 1-59052-465-9, $24.99

→ [Adam + R] — talk can grandmother of W-B

  — see baby next week

→ Dan — wenddm

→ Mindy + Dom —

→ (Adam —) anger